FACES OF CHRISTMAS PAST

FACES OF CHRISTMAS PAST

BILL HOLM

Afton Historical Society Press
Afton, Minnesota

Cover photograph: Six-year-old Bill Holm as Hopalong Cassidy,
Christmas 1949

Library of Congress Cataloging-in-Publication Data
Holm, Bill, 1943–
    Faces of Christmas past / Bill Holm.
        p.   cm.
    ISBN 1-890434-02-7
    1. Christmas--United States.   2. Christmas--Iceland.   I. Title.
    GT4986.A1H65   1997   97-26943
    394.2663 ' 0973--dc21   CIP

Material from *The Island Man* by Tomás Ó'Crohan, originally published
in 1934, is used by permission of Oxford University Press.

Printed in Canada

The Afton Historical Society Press is a non-profit organization that
takes great pride and pleasure in publishing fine books on Minnesota
subjects.

W. Duncan MacMillan   Patricia Condon Johnston
president   publisher

AFTON HISTORICAL SOCIETY PRESS
P.O. Box 100
Afton, MN 55001
1-800-436-8443

*M*y interior Christmas begins early, sometimes the first snow in October, sometimes the last scorcher in August. The Christmas letter rears up in the mind's eye like a sudden thunderhead in a bright sky. I imagine the rummaging through drawers for last year's pile of Christmas cards and the attempt at rationalizing my way into an escape: "Why bother? No one reads them. I don't have time for this. I haven't seen some of these people in years. Others don't bother. (I make a list.)

It's a silly habit; habits can be tamed and broken." The whine goes on. The excuses don't work.

During the first blizzard, I rummage, find not only last year's Christmas cards (a sizable lump), but the last ten years', maybe twenty. Some senders are now dead from inevitable age or bad luck. Some are divorced, some re-married, some not; some simply moved or disappeared. At Christmas, we want steadiness, a still point in a chaotic world, but we get mutability, a mirror with the face of chaos staring back at us.

In the second blizzard, I brood and examine my own character, my passing life. I cross-examine it, send it to the interior jury, convict it, sentence it—if not to death, at least to exile. But either mercy or lethargy or both reprieve it. Of what am I guilty? Of being silly and weak, a procrastinator, a carrier-out of orders from the dead, a skeptical practitioner of ritual, of having arrived at middle age without entirely finishing youth. Thus I am guilty of being human, more normal than I imagine in my more grandiose moments.

By the third blizzard, I am steeled to the job, lashed to the grim wheel of duty. Since recent Minnesota blizzards have been the three- or four-day variety with howling hurricane winds—the world invisible inside a maelstrom of snow and wind-chills lethal enough to finish you off in two or three minutes—there's not much else to do except your duty. I write the Christmas essay, a half whimsical, half melancholy sermon on the progress of another year, set out the sheets of stamps and boxes of envelopes, arrange the pens next to the pile of cards, stare wistfully out the kitchen window at the icy white scrim over the universe, and begin. Merry Christmas . . .

$\mathcal{W}$hat, you might ask, am I doing with ten or twenty years of old Christmas cards? For all I know, fifty-year-old cards may lurk in unopened boxes. At thirty-two, I found myself heir to my mother's and father's lifetime accumulations of stuff too valued to be thrown: old tools, photographs, boxes of crocheting, knitting, wood painting, every toy I ever played with, and every scribble of paper in my handwriting—childish poems, school essays, letters. I was an adored only child, but this—this was ridiculous! At the back of a closet sat a shoebox full of baby congratulations cards—from 1943.

Jona and Big Bill were both devoted pack rats. Raised without money in Icelandic immigrant farm families, they married in 1932 to slog through the whole Depression trying to buy back my grandfather's farm from a loan company. They narrowly escaped foreclosure, hanging tenaciously onto the old Holm farm at the edge of the Dust Bowl until World War II, Minnesota Governor Floyd B. Olson and FDR saved them. One consequence of that chronology was the inability to get rid of anything that they actually owned. Neither of them was thrifty with money; rather they practiced mad generosity to friends, strangers, and of course to me, the beloved child. But a broken hayrake or iron tractor wheel, or a bag of holey nylon stockings, patched underwear, paper-thin overalls, and moth-eaten sweaters was different. They could be recycled, made useful, given new life, like half-gone leftovers disappearing into a hot dish. I once wrote a poem about my mother's habit with these lines:

> *Your never know, she said*
> *when it might come in handy,*
> *and you can always put it in the soup*
> *where it'll taste good.*

After more than twenty years of overseeing the Holm ancestral junk, I look around appalled to find that not only have I thrown almost nothing, I have instead doubled the holdings. I am a genetic pack rat with a weakness for paper, not iron or craft supplies. Books, magazines, letters, musical scores, manuscripts, and old Christmas cards have eaten wall space, corners, window ledges, the floor up to the bed springs.

The ritual of the Christmas card list is a visible emblem of spiritual packrattery. Going through my mother's boxes after she died in 1975, I found her collection of old cards. What to do? I added my mother's list to my already sizable accumulation: more cousins, uncles, aunts, old neighbors, her stamp pals, schoolmates. After twenty years, the old family list shrunk though the attrition of death, but new cousins surfaced, new connections from strange parts of the world where I've lived and worked, old friends with grown children who have themselves become friends. My December duty now resembles Jacob Marley's chains. They rattle after me wherever I go.

But the Christmas letter is only half a burden. It is also a necessity, even a pleasure. No matter the awkwardness of tone or expression—Christmas letters are often comically guilty of two great human failings: bragging and complaining—its real message lives under the language. I am alive, it says, still on the planet. I have not forgotten you. The thread, whether of blood, nostalgia or friendship, that sews us together has not been cut. In a culture Balkanized by technology and groupthink, the Christmas letter is a human message in an envelope bottle, a small ritual where we name each other one at a time, even if only in a scribbled sentence at the bottom of a Xerox.

The old cliché to the contrary, a picture is probably not worth a thousand words. Language, like music, takes time; a picture slaps us in the face in an instant. It hardens and makes plain what language can sometimes soften and make subtle. Some find escape from an annual Christmas essay by sending the Christmas card snapshot with a cheery but brief printed greeting. I have never sunk to it. I take my photographs with sentences. But at the bottom of a dusty box of family memorabilia, I found evidence that my mother and father swallowed the whole bait—for years sending out "cute" photographs of their long-awaited single son. The sequence begins in the mid-forties, continuing until the mid-fifties. By then, teenage acne and surliness robbed the photographs of their "cuteness," so Jona and Bill retreated to Hallmark and hand-written notes.

I don't remember ever seeing those photos as a child. When I first found them, at about forty, I chuckled at the grotesque little boy who certainly didn't seem to have much connection to me as a grown man. But now, past fifty and barely recognizable as this dimpled young fellow, I realize with a kind of ironic dismay that I still contain the little cowboy of 1949. He's duded up with his Hopalong Cassidy outfit: chaps, six-gun in holster, bandanna, and Suzuki-size ten gallon hat, ready to fast draw on the photographer, proclaiming in his soprano grumble, "Stick 'em up!" My hand already clutches the gun. In 1950 the seven-year-old goose hunter sends "Seasons Greetings": Big Bill's twelve-gauge 1897 Remington pump in one hand and the neck of a dead

Canadian honker in the other. The next year features
the solemn boy in a floral shirt standing in front of the
family's new brown Dodge, asphyxiating Andrew, the
white barn cat. The cat, with terrified eyes and flat ears,
looks ready to claw the boy and leap for freedom. In
1952 same boy, same shirt, but now he's squeezing an
alarmed rabbit. Thick black spectacles adorn his pink
nose. He's on his way to junior high nerd king!

No printed letter accompanies these cards depicting
the progress of Little Billy. In time, the gun slinger and
goose hunter grew up to be a devout pacifist who spent
his twenties "clean for Gene" marching against Lyndon
Johnson's war. The pet choker grew up to think that ani-
mals deserve to stay wild and outdoors. These Christmas
photos announce to me (and to you, since your face probably appeared on similar cards) that I most certainly am

not eternal, but that some stubborn core of character born early will last until my own death, whether I want it or not.

On December 22, 1996, the *Sioux Falls Argus Leader's* travel columnist, Anson Yeager, published an essay on Christmas photo cards that takes a cheerier view than mine. *Here's a tip* [he wrote] *for young couples who want a Christmas card and pictorial history in one package. Make your Christmas card a family picture of some significant event during the year. Continue with a new card every year as your children grow up and you become grandparents. My wife and I last week mailed our 44th picture Christmas card since 1952. . . .*

We switched from black and white to color pictures in 1980. There were graduations, weddings, and new faces of daughters-in-law on the cards.

Grandchildren followed. . . . Picture taking has become easier. My automatic Japanese camera rarely misses a good shot. [In 1990, the Yeager clan] *donned western gear—from frontier army uniforms to dance hall girl costumes—during our . . . summer reunion . . . near Mt. Rushmore. . . . One recent Christmas Ada May gave each child a photo album of cards. They said it was one of their nicest gifts ever.*

Now there's Americana! All the right buttons buzzed at once: history, tradition, family, good humored kitsch and clowning around, and a coffee table conversation starter to boot. But we do our superior clucking at some peril to our souls. That Christmas photograph album is a rite, and as humans have been assured by Confucius and every sane philosopher since: "He who can submit himself to ritual is Good. If (a ruler) could for one day 'himself submit to ritual,' everyone under Heaven would respond to his Goodness."

One conspicuous omission in Mr. Yeager's breezy view of a nice Christmas gift is that no one is dead yet in his forty-four years of snapshots so no one remembers or imagines the absent faces staring into a near half century deep chasm. Christmas cards should weep a little too. Americans love cheerfulness, pep, the old can-do spirit, but it afflicts us with a kind of deliberate unconsciousness to the civilizing power of ritual. We cannot have the yang without the yin, as Confucius's contemporary Lao Tze reminds us. Otherwise we grow into only half a human, trapped in an imaginary golden (or leaden) childhood. The boy still lives, but heavier now, not only according to a bathroom scale. This bit of cautionary moralizing will not affect the arrival next year of one hundred per cent of the photo cards from your friends adorned with gleaming teeth and countenances of pure buoyant good cheer. Smile, it's Christmas!

🎄🎄🎄

*A*t Christmas, the gavel of tradition bangs on the table to call the house to order. We have always done it this way, so do it now. We have always eaten—oysters, lutefisk, ham balls, fill in the blank—so we shall eat them again. In towns like Minneota, the solid front of Christmas habit brought even the atheists to church on Christmas Eve. The Jewish doctor's children acted in the Sunday school Christmas pageant. A Hindu could not have escaped appearing in the manger scene, toasting the holiday afterwards with garishly decorated butter cookies dunked in thin coffee.

Yet tradition, anywhere in America (and certainly in the Midwest) is a strangely jackleg affair, hardly old enough to qualify as tradition at all, rather only invented procedure. A tradition must be so old that its true origin, while lost to us consciously, remains quick inside the cells of the body. Tradition grows from the texture of the grass, the shape of the hills, the color of rivers when the snow melts, the swampy pasture where our great-grandfather's horse stumbled and broke his leg. We haven't been long enough in Minneota to earn that kind of tradition.

But what about the old country, you ask? Didn't tradition travel over on the boat from Ireland, Norway, Iceland, Belgium? A majority of Minneotans descend from those stocks, hardly over a century ago. But traditions seem not to travel well over water; most sickened in mid-Atlantic and expired shortly after they stepped off the horse cart onto the tall grass prairie. This is a country of interrupted traditions, just entering a difficult puberty to start growing real ones. The physician poet, William Carlos Williams, described us well, if a little harshly, as "tricked out . . . /with gauds/ from imaginations which have no/ peasant traditions to give them/ character . . ."

But at Christmas, my mother, Jona, "tricked out" her house with gauds that would have astonished even Dr. Williams, and as she would have briskly assured him, she had plenty of character. She might have defined tradition as anything you did once that looked good to you, so you practiced it forty or fifty times more—and behold you have invented "tradition."

Jona and Big Bill Holm

Jonina Sigurborg Josephson Holm, my mother, was a woman of extraordinary energy and vitality. In her, the life force was not an idea but an eruption. Born in 1910 on a farm to parents who spoke little or no English, she longed for education, travel, adventure, the Big World. She escaped all of seven miles south to Minneota to graduate from high school, worked in Leland's Drug Store illegally filling prescriptions, and in 1932, after years of his courting and cajoling, married Bill Holm, her childhood sweetheart, to return seven miles north to yet another immigrant farm only a few miles from her parents. No college, no career, no New York—not even Minneapolis, half a lifetime away on mud roads. Just an unpaid-for farm, a drafty shack of a house, kerosene lamps, a pump over the sink, and a two-holer outhouse. These bare details of her life are not peculiar; her story is the story of a million women of her generation in the rural United States—and probably in the big cities too, though school was easier there.

Like most of that million, she didn't whine. If luck and circumstance thwarted her longing for beauty, elegance, an exciting life, she would act out her longing by inventing her own version of them wherever she was. Without having any idea what "art" or "taste" were, she possessed, probably from birth, the equipment of an artist; a skilled hand, a sharp eye, a willingness to make mistakes, and mammoth reserves of energy. She crocheted, she knitted, she embroidered, she painted figurines and wooden plates and breadboards, she made ceramic ashtrays, lamps, bowls, casserole dishes, she glued beads and gewgaws on any recyclable object, however unlikely, she canned and baked and pickled, she collected stamps, hand ruling the pages with a Parker fountain pen after checking her perforation gauge, she sewed dresses, shirts, coats, and when they wore thin, she adorned them with decorative patches, and then patches on top of the patches. Whatever interested her at any given moment, she surrendered to in excess. Without ever having heard of William Blake, she practiced his maxim by instinct: *The road of excess leads to the palace of wisdom.* When wooden plates captured her attention she painted fifty for relatives, fifty for neighbors and friends, fifty to sell (though mostly she gave them away), and another fifty for storage under the bed, just in case. Not only was her enthusiasm contagious, she owned no resistance to the enthusiasms of others. If a neighbor learned from the radio or a crafts magazine how to make pink swan soap dishes out of plastic dish soap bottles, Jona swung into action and tried a few hundred herself. None of her projects, however, intruded into the time she spent on her real passion: human beings—creatures capable of language and conversation, the telling of stories. She entered a room talking, eyed the company to see who might need cheering up, finishing the sentence when she closed the door behind her. When she died, one of her friends, amazed that death had been tough or fast enough to do Jona in, sighed and said, "She had only two speeds, high and off."

Her house became the gallery for her projects, and at Christmas, her favorite season, the show doubled or tripled in size to overwhelm the cramped little farmstead. Out came the boxes of handmade tree ornaments, the painted figurines of Santa and his whole retinue—reindeer, elves, sleighs, a set of wise men and camels and an electrified manger scene with blinking lights, angels of various color and design, dishes and bowls decorated with poinsettias and mistletoe, the embroidered Christmas tablecloth and napkins, the rosemaled napkin rings, wooden plates painted with Christmas motifs and Yuletide greetings in four or five languages, Christmas bric-a-brac on every flat surface, handmade candle holders of maybe fifteen designs with scented candles burned nightly for a month, their smells of lavender sachet, pine forest, and spicy cinnamon oozing together in the drafty rooms, and finally, my favorites, the Christmas angels made from folded magazines shellacked and spray painted to a board-like stiffness, and the *piece-de-resistance:* the Christmas toilet seat cover with a gay red winking Santa Claus waiting for your hind end (this came after acquiring a flush toilet in 1950).

And it was a house of "gauds"; no subtle earth tones or delicate pastels for Jona—she loved bright, intense, gypsy color: red, hot pink, purple, orange, gold, lime green. These wise men had *style*; these angels played tambourines, not ethereal harps. In a bleak old farmhouse on the bleak north crest of a bleak hill on a bleak prairie with the bleakest climate on the continent, this house, inhabited by Scandinavian Lutherans, looked like a Hungarian restaurant decorated for a Chinese wedding.

My mother cared little for the theology of Christmas. She was, at best, a nominal Lutheran, faithful to Ladies' Aid and do-good projects but casual in her piety. Her Christmas music consisted of breathy performances of *Heim Sem Bol* (*Silent Night* in Icelandic) and *Jingle Bells* on a Hohner harmonica—and this only after a well laced Tom-and-Jerry or two. She loved the festivity of Christmas, the chance to create some light and noise and gaiety at the bottom of the year's darkness, cold, and silence. If you had to live in this godforsaken place at least show some evidence of being actually alive. Maybe that's the real kernel of psychological wisdom underlying the Christmas rites anyway. Jona's extroverted nature guided her to stumble into that wisdom unconsciously.

What she made was not "kitsch"; kitsch implies a consciousness of fashionable taste satirically undermined. Jona invented beauty—as she understood it. Her creations connected not so much to her ego as to her affectionate desire to please others. If you admired a piece of her handiwork, you went home with it. As a boy, sometimes overwhelmed by the crowded gypsy camp atmosphere inside the house at Christmas, I kept wishing for more traffic, more guests to do a little thinning and pruning on the collection. It would have done no good; she would simply have swung into action and invented more. The Icelandic Christmas tradition inside her family and immigrant culture evaporated in the new world, except for a few Christmas recipes that were adaptations of food that had already begun to disappear from real old country tables. One ritual function of a tradition is to create connection inside a community. So, lacking Iceland, Jona made do, announcing: "This is now tradition; help yourself."

I traveled to Iceland as a Fulbright professor in 1978 to teach American literature. I also wanted to find what my relatives had left behind when they moved to North America. They'd left Christmas, for one thing. Two Yuletides in Iceland taught me something about the sentimentalizing of holidays in America. Christmas still generates a little terror in Iceland. All cheer and no fear take the edge off our Christmas fun.

At almost 66 degrees north, not much sun arrives in Reykjavík in December, only a few hours of slant gray light that slithers over the mountains. Keep your car lights on and your lamps lit. Somewhere at the edges of the island, old glaciers grind down inexorably toward the sea in pitch darkness. Volcanoes simmer under that ice. Not far away. Close.

Icelanders, while not overtly religious, are superstitious, just in case. To believe that the dead remain present in a landscape seems a mark of civilization to them.

To practice the rites, you must use memory and invite the dead, whether you love or fear them, to join.

It's probably no surprise that the best Icelandic ghost stories I heard take place on Christmas Eve. The Deacon of Myrká (dark) Church arranges to pick up his girlfriend, Guðrun, a hired girl on a neighborhood farm, on his gray horse, Faxi, to ride to Christmas vespers. Since he has drowned in a glacial river a few days before, he's a little late picking up Guðrun, and he doesn't say much. With an icy hand, he hoists her brusquely onto Faxi and rides off with her through the frozen valley. The moon scuds through a cloud strewn sky, sometimes giving a little light. When Faxi plunges down a steep bank to ford a river, the Deacon's hat lifts slightly. As the moon drifts from under a cloud, Guðrun sees the bare skull. The Deacon croons:

The moon is gliding;

Death is riding.

See the white fleck

At the back of my neck,

Garoon-Garoon.

Having joined the undead, the Deacon can no longer pronounce Guðrun's name, since the first three letters spell the Icelandic name of God. Guðrun is terrified, but what can she do? The horse gallops wildly to the church gate. In the church yard, Guðrun sees an open grave surrounded by a pile of freshly dug dirt. The Deacon leaps from Faxi's back and grabs Guðrun's riding cloak in his bony grip. She left home in such a hurry that she put only one arm in her cloak. Clutching the empty cloak the Deacon leaps into the open grave while the piles of heaped dirt scamper down into the hole to cover him. The pastor came later to sing Psalms for the shaken Guðrun, but as the story reports, she was never quite the same. A sorcerer had to be summoned to cast spells and roll a boulder over the Deacon's grave to keep his ghost quiet. Merry Christmas. Gleðileg Jól.

Instead of the kindly, benevolent, pink-cheeked, blubbery old coot of a Santa Claus who squeezes down chimneys to satisfy consumer cravings of spoiled bourgeois children, the Icelanders enjoyed the thirteen Christmas trolls—the Jólasveinar. Their names and the literal translations are too grand and strange to leave only to the Icelanders. Here's the lot of them. Pronounce fearlessly. Neglect no consonant!

1. Stekkjastaur   Sheep-Cot Clod

2. Giljagaur   Gully Gawk

3. Stúfur   Shorty

4. Thvörusleikir	Ladle Licker
5. Pottasleikir	Pot Scraper
6. Askasleikir	Bowl Licker
7. Hurðaskellir	Door Slammer
8. Skyrgámur	Skyr Gobbler
9. Bjúgnakrækir	Sausage Swiper
10. Gluggagægir	Window Peeper
11. Gáttathefur	Door Sniffer
12. Ketkrókur	Meat Hook
13. Kertasníkir	Candle Beggar

They live in the mountains (a fierce prospect in Iceland; the interior mountains are uninhabitable lava crags that resemble the surface of the moon) and begin appearing at farms and towns one per day, thirteen days before Christmas. They also leave one per day thus making Christmas a twenty-six-day white knuckler for worried children. These trolls eat naughty children or steal them back to the mountains for God knows what horrors. Behave! Or else!

The trolls come by their foul natures honestly, born out of wedlock (of course!) to troll parents named Grýla and Leppalúði. The misshapen ogress, Grýla, comes from an ancient dark corner of the Norse mind, the Viking Tooth Mother. She is named in the old *Eddas* and described in the *Saga of Icelanders*:

> *Here goes Grýla*
> *by the farm*
> *and from her hang*
> *fourteen tails.*
> *On every tail*
> *a hundred bags,*
> *in every bag*
> *are twenty brats.*

She wakes the boys, the Jólasveinnar, before Christmas, sending them down to fetch children for her always brewing pot. If you have seen one of the "cute" little Norse elves in Christmas gift shops, steal yourself for Grýla's face and cackle. She is your nightmare.

If they escape the clutches of Grýla and her gang, Icelanders generally spend a quiet Christmas Eve with their relatives, eating smoked mutton, creamed potatoes and peas washed down with coffee—or for the urbane, a bottle of wine. After too many layered cream cakes and sweet breads, they open presents, yawn, then drift off to sleep listening to the wind from Greenland howl while they dream of beaches in Spain. Maybe my mother should have moved back to the old country to bring a little pizzazz and color to the Icelandic Christmas or at least cover the toilet seats with something to amuse the bad-tempered trolls on their nightly visits. Tradition can move in two directions, after all.

♣ ♣ ♣

J oughtn't to make harsh remarks about Santa Claus, since judging by the mirror, my outer shell has grown into him; the little cowboy progresses in middle age to Jolly Old St. Nicholas. Once red hair and pale cheeks, now red cheeks and pale hair with a properly jolly belly for good measure. I went to Madagascar early in 1997, as far from Minneota as you can travel, and as foreign a place as exists on the planet. I walked through the market in Antananarivo, sweating in the heat of a tropical summer, accompanied by gangs of golden skinned, bare-footed children who addressed me jovially and loudly as "Pere Noel." I have metamorphosed into a cliché, or to put a more kindly construction on my fate, entered into tradition by virtue of biology as destiny.

But my destiny was not to work in a department store getting a wet lap and having my beard tugged. I loved neither the giving nor the receiving of conventional gifts. My connection to the tradition and rites of Christmas, from childhood until now, came from the chance it offered to sing, play, and hear wonderful music, and have read to me the resonant cadences of the *King James Bible*, whose language remains sublime verbal music in my ear. My Christmas duty to my neighbors and my community consisted in refusing no chance to perform music.

Christmas music presents us with an odd paradox. In the presumed season of good will, good cheer, and buoyant optimism, much of the greatest music is sad, inward, and reflective. Sometimes we bowdlerize that feeling (for whatever motives) in order to thump a tune or poem that ought to quiet us. When I was a boy soprano, I loved singing the setting of Longfellow's poem: "Christmas Bells." In every hymnal I've examined, it's printed with four stanzas. The last verse begins oddly with a "then" that makes no grammatical sense in the context of the first three. For years I credited this to Longfellow's shortcomings as a poet, and his tiresome "Tell me not in mournful numbers" upbeat cheeriness. Last year, browsing though his complete works, I discovered to my surprise seven stanzas in the poem.

CHRISTMAS BELLS

I heard the bells on Christmas Day
Their old, familiar carols play,
And wild and sweet
The words repeat
Of peace on earth, good-will to men!

And thought how, as the day had come,
The belfries of all Christendom
Had rolled along
The unbroken song
Of peace on earth, good-will to men!

Till, ringing, singing on its way,
The world revolved from night to day,
A voice, a chime,
A chant sublime
Of peace on earth, good-will to men!

Then from each black, accursed mouth
The cannon thundered in the South,
And with the sound
The carols drowned
Of peace on earth, good-will to men!

It was as if an earthquake rent
The hearth-stones of a continent,
And made forlorn
The households born
Of peace on earth, good-will to men!

And in despair I bowed my head;
"There is no peace on earth," I said;
"For hate is strong,
And mocks the song
Of peace on earth, good-will to men!"

Then pealed the bells more loud and deep;
God is not dead; nor doth he sleep!
The Wrong shall fail,
The Right prevail,
With peace on earth, good-will to men!

With stanzas four, five, and six restored, and the poem's date, 1863, revealed, the Civil War barges into the Christmas rites to upset the decorum of Christmas sentiment. The poem deepens; the earnest Victorian tune deepens too. Try singing it with all seven verses. Two new guests enter the church; history and human nature (so often left shivering in the snow outside the church door) take their seats to join the congregation. Longfellow's trumpet blat assertion: "The Wrong shall fail/ The Right prevail," still seems hollow. We'll see about prevailing as time goes on, and also see if humans can think clearly about moral categories without capital letters and exclamation points. But the lost stanzas restore the honor of the rite.

Christina Rossetti brings cold and poverty into the church on Christmas Eve. Her poem, "In the Bleak

Mid-winter," most famously set by Gustav Holst, proved irresistible to other composers too. All the tunes are lovely and quiet as if the poem itself insisted on quality in the notes it wears.

> *In the bleak midwinter*
> *Frosty winds made moan,*
> *Earth stood hard as iron,*
> *Water like a stone.*
> *Snow had fallen, snow on snow,*
> *Snow . . . on . . . snow,*
> *In the bleak midwinter,*
> *Long ago.*

How well Minnesotans understand lines five and six! Snow seems to begin falling inside the language of the stanza. The poem ends:

What can I give him,

Poor as I am?

If I were a shepherd,

I would bring a lamb;

If I were a wise man,

I would do my part;

Yet what can I give him—

Give my heart.

Try that, sung sotto voce, in a candle lit church on Christmas Eve. Eyes will moisten in the pews. At last, after the tinsel and toasting, we are all cold and poor, and some part longs to have the news sung to us.

Sometimes, perhaps during a December blizzard, I celebrate a private Christmas by playing odd pieces on the piano for an hour or two. Bach, Handel, Christmas carols? No, I play the Christmas pieces of Franz Liszt and Ferruccio Busoni, two of grandest virtuosos of the last century and this, respectively, both famous for producing tidal waves of sound, pages black with notes. But their Christmas pieces are instead austere, quiet, reflective, simple and heartfelt. The piano hardly rises above pianissimo; sometimes the notes seem to disappear into wind, snow, and silence.

Liszt, whatever his mistaken reputation as rake and bounder, was a tender and devoted father and grandfather. In his mid-sixties, he wrote a set of Christmas pieces called *Weihnachtsbaum* (Christmas Tree Suite), dedicated to his granddaughter Daniela. Two of his children died young; his possibility for marriage and domestic life was finally frustrated. Like any man in his mid-sixties, he reflected on his own childhood and past Christmases. The twelve pieces, while not "easy," can be managed by amateurs, the notes few and thin, the mood thoughtful and inward. He resets a few old carols—a medieval chant, *In Dulci Jubilo* and *Adeste Fidelis* among them—writes a few Christmas bell pieces, a cradle song, reminiscences of places he has lived, songs he's heard. I think *Ehemals* (Formerly) the saddest four pages of Liszt. In this dreamy waltz a man of complicated character meditates on what is lost and irretrievable in his sixty-five Christmases. The music shrinks to a single line, then only a note or two played with a single finger, then silence. If you own a piano, play it yourself, however well you can manage it. After it takes shape under your hands, play it for someone you love in a half dark room.

Busoni dedicates *Sonatina In Diem Nativitatus Christi MCMXVII* to his son Benvenuto, a soldier in World War I. Like most European intellectuals, Busoni saw the whole of his civilization collapsing around him in a heap of gun powder, trench mud, mustard gas, and patriotic cant, while his own much loved son dodged bullets fired for no sane end. He thus composes his most serene and lucid music, full of the tolling of sad bells, half-heard carols, and in the closing passages, directs that the music be played *quasi transfigurato*—as if transfigured. If civilization insisted on destroying itself with blood lust, Busoni would hold his small corner together with order and calm, a fragment shored against the ruin of Europe, a hope that the ancient Christmas ritual survive the mindless savagery of war.

There is my little concert for you to play at home or offer as a Christmas gift, a couple of hymns and a few sad piano pieces by unlikely composers. You have your own private list of Christmas music that moves you—-maybe the boys of Kings College singing the floating descant above *Once in Royal David's City*, maybe Bing Crosby singing *White Christmas*. It makes no difference. They are gifts to you; give them away. Share the rite.

Winter 1996-97, a humdinger, started early, bore down hard, and persisted. In mid-May, as I write these sentences, its ghost still lingers: frost warnings tonight, withered tulips, piles of tree debris from huge ice storms seven months ago. Grand Forks, North Dakota, a city of fifty thousand, disappeared under snow melt and fire. A Minneota citizen did me no favor by counting: "Seventeen blizzards, and that's just the big ones when they closed all the highways." You don't want to know some things. For the first time in anyone's memo-ry, all of the local churches were closed on Christmas Eve and Christmas Day. The music was provided by 70 mph winds driving horizontal snow through the window case-ments. I had plenty of time to rummage, brood, and pro-crastinate on my way to writing the annual Christmas let-ter. I'll give you the first page so that you can participate in the flavor of this annual ceremony.

Dear Friends,

I begin this letter in Pierre, SD, at the Governors Inn on December 17. Outside the window, wind gusts up to 50 or 60 mph swirl the snow into a white rage. A few neon lights from gas stations and fast food joints remain foggily visible as through a veil. Outside town, nothing, the world a blank, invisible emptiness of whirling snow, the only sounds:

the twanging of fences, the rattling of car win-
dows, and unearthly howling from the north
wind like the cries of some prehistoric carni-
vore hungry for its last meal. That meal might
be you, if you are foolish enough to try the
road. At wind-chills of more than -60 degrees
Fahrenheit, exposed flesh begins freezing in
less than 90 seconds. But you can't leave
Pierre anyway. The road south to the inter-
state is blocked by a sideways UPS truck that
collided with a disabled car. Then the inter-
state is closed. Here you are, not where you
want to be at all, but where nature and chance
leave you. I'm here because I'm reading
poems with South Dakota Acoustic Christmas,
a traveling concert with a dozen wonderful
musicians. We left Rapid City yesterday in a
complete white-out creeping along the 200
miles to Pierre at 15 or 20 mph, sometimes

stopped completely looking for a yellow line. Amazingly, all dozen of us made it.

Five hundred assembled for a concert at the big fancy theater at Pierre high school. Local folks almost filled the hall, despite the foul night. Five minutes before the opening number, the hall plunged into darkness, only a few dim emergency bulbs. The city trans- former out, the whole town black . . . no heat . . . no mikes . . . no big heavy sound system. Well, we're acoustic. The show went on in the semi-darkness, a few flashlights from the balcony lighting up the performers. Without amplification, the audience had to listen actively to fiddle, guitar, mandolin, voice. That listening had a skin on it! The music was alive, as artificially loud noises can never be. Night vision took over and faces became visible. They glowed in the soft light. Screw electricity, I thought. We've never needed it. It's made babies, fools and whiners of us. That high school theater in Pierre reminded me of China where machines and technology dependably failed and life went on anyway without fuss. That transformer is just a crutch. Throw it away and be healed! Walk! And your car won't get you far either when the road is invisible and leads only to fast death.

Midwesterners always start conversations with weather reports, boring both themselves and innocent outlanders; but maybe it's their way of clanging an interior reminder that nature is larger than your opinions, your plans, your achievements, your accumulations. Sometimes citizens of a rich country in the "information age" forget that. An Arctic blizzard is bigger than cyberspace.

The musicians spent the next two and a half days at the Governors Inn waiting for the wind to calm down. They twanged guitars, practiced their mandolin licks, visited relatives and old friends who lived in the navigable ten block radius of the motel, drank a little whiskey and beer, worried about their Christmas plans and their teenaged children left home alone. There are worse companions in a Christmas blizzard than musicians. We finally performed five more concerts but none touched the quality—even the grandeur—of that glorious, quiet music in a dark house.

*H*uman beings have proved their capacity to survive suffering, bad luck, poverty, isolation, natural disasters. Christ did, after all, and that's one of the rites we celebrate for each other at Christmas. We age and we die (old Christmas photos provide evidence), but we think about it, and at our best, sing about it. Christmas, much more than New Year's Eve, is the ritual that asks us to take stock, remember, allow our minds and consciences to be flooded with our own history. If we are honest, this will not lead us to back-slapping cheeriness, but it might bring us the quiet joy that we have done our job as human beings by living out our lives, however many Christmases we have marked off on the calendar. The little cowboy of 1949 still sends me interior Christmas cards, so I humor him by putting up my hands, saying "I surrender": to age, the passage of time, what cannot be fixed in this world, maybe to the necessary rites of civilization.

As a benediction for this Christmas essay, I offer an Irish story about Christmas Eve and the power of music.

It was written in Irish about 1920 by an unschooled fisherman named Tomás Ó'Crohan, one of the last inhabitants of the Blasket Islands, wave battered specks of inhospitable rock in the stormy Atlantic west of the Dingle peninsula. As with all great stories, and all great lives, notice that this one ends with singing.

> *When the time for lighting up came on*
> *"God's Blessed Eve," if you were coming*
> *towards the village from the south-east—*
> *for that's the direction in which every door*
> *and window faces—and every kind of light*
> *is ablaze that night, you would imagine it*
> *a wing of some heavenly mansion, though*
> *it is set in the middle of the great sea. You*
> *would hear a noise in every house that*
> *night, for, however much or little drink*

comes to the Island, it is put aside for Christmas Eve. Maybe an old man would be singing who'd never lifted his voice for a year. As for the old women, they're always lilting away.

I felt that I would rather go out a bit than spend the whole evening at home. The place I meant to go to was Pats Heamish's house for a bit, for he wasn't too well yet. I knew that he hadn't got a drop of drink, so I got a half-pint. There was a score or so of welcomes waiting for me. He was a man you could get a great deal of sport out of, but he was anything but happy, as he hadn't got a drop for Christmas. He'd drunk up all that he'd brought with him from Dingle, as his health *had gone to pieces after the carouse.*

I handed him the half-pint.

"Drink that down," said I to him, "for you've got to sing a song."

"You'll get no song," says Kate, "if he once gets the half-pint down."

"I'll sing a song, too," says Tom.

He drank a tot and sang, not one song, but seven of them.

Tomás and I wish you all seven songs. May you never fall into the clutches of Grýla. May you cultivate virtue. May you keep the rites of civilization in your own house in your own way on Christmas Eve, whenever it falls in your life.

BIOGRAPHY

Bill Holm was born in 1943 in Minneota, Minnesota, and, after an absence of twenty years, lives there again. He teaches in the English Department at Southwest State University in Marshall, Minnesota, part of the year; the rest of the year he travels—sometimes to Madagascar, sometimes to South Dakota, practices on the piano, harpsichord, and clavichord, and writes. He is the author of six books, two of poetry and four of prose. *Landscape of Ghosts* (1993), with photographer Bob Firth, explores the prairie landscape that is often the scene of his essays. In his last book, *The Heart Can Be Filled Anywhere on Earth* (1996), he tells stories of immigrant Icelanders in his hometown of Minneota. Like Zorba, he will have to live to be a thousand years old to finish reading the piles of books that cram his TV- and computer-free house, and to travel to the strange places that have roused his curiosity. He may give up the Christmas letters any year now.

Designed by
Barbara J. Arney
Stillwater, MN

Typefaces are
Bodoni & ExPonto